T0154989

STREET
fighting

Consistently throughout this very fine first book of poems is a precision of diction and an almost impeccable care for words that has the power to lift these poems, and the lives that inhabit them, somehow off the page, and then deep into our brains. I like too the unusual and engaging angle of vision of these poems, a lingering seductive kind of observation characterized most accurately by Mr. Donaghy's own words: "Often we cannot read the gesture/ until the figure becomes background." This is an entertaining book that is a true joy to read.

–Bruce Weigl

In *Streetfighting* Daniel Donaghy writes unswervingly about a gritty urban environment, and what in a lesser talent would have been simply depressing, a mother smearing her son's face with a crushed lightning bug, or a boy falling from a high catwalk, "so quietly/ no one else knew he was gone," we find instead small acts of courage and compassion, even a kind of grace achieved while playing basketball and street baseball, and most importantly a coming-to-terms with the past, with parents, with wrongs committed. Donaghy has more than enough talent and wisdom to pull it off in this brilliant debut collection.

–Harry Humes

STREET *fighting* POEMS

"York and Clarion Streets, Philadelphia." –**Martin J. Desht**

DANIEL DONAGHY

BkMk Press
University of Missouri-Kansas City

Copyright © 2005 by Daniel Donaghy

BkMk Press
University of Missouri-Kansas City
5101 Rockhill Road
Kansas City, Missouri 64110
(816) 235-2558 (voice)
(816) 235-2611 (fax)
bkmk@umkc.edu
www.umkc.edu/bkmk

Cover and book design: Cody Lynn Rinehart
Cover photo: Martin J. Desht
Author photo: Karen Donaghy
Production Staff: Ben Furnish (managing editor), Susan L.
   Schurman (assistant managing editor), Michelle Boisseau
   (associate editor), Bill Beeson, J.J. Cantrell
Printing: Technical Communication Services, North Kansas City, Missouri

Financial assistance for this project was provided by
the Missouri Arts Council, a state agency.

Library of Congress Cataloging-in-Publication Data

Donaghy, Daniel,
      Streetfighting / by Daniel Donaghy.
            p. cm.
      ISBN 1886157499   (pbk.: alk. paper)   1. Young men—Poetry
   2. Irish American families—Poetry   3. Fathers—Death—Poetry
   4. Poor families—Poetry   5. Catholics—Poetry
   6. Philadelphia (Pa.)—Poetry

   PS3604.O+S+
                                          200428595

This book is set in Stencil, Sand, and Myriad type.

for Karen and Abigail

ACKNOWLEDGMENTS

Alaska Quarterly Review: "Jimmy"

Allegheny Review: "Shrapnel"

Beacon Street Review: "Snow Hitchers," "You and Irene"

Chaminade Literary Review: "Felix and the School Desk,"
        "Heartwood"

Cimarron Review: "Conversion"

Commonweal: "Digging for Summer: 1986"

HazMat Review: "The Years Without Understanding"

Image: "The Nature of Memory and Fireflies"

The MacGuffin: "Snapshot"

New Letters: "Christmas," "George," "One Thing That Didn't Make
        the Papers," "The One Time I Paid Attention at Friday
        Morning Mass," "Things Like This Happen All the Time,"
        "Timmy's Eye"

Oasis: "Ant Town"

One Trick Pony: "Three Houses, Three Dogs"

Organica: "Halfies in Philadelphia and the Ritual of Desire,"
        "The Someone Everyone Knows," "Elegy for T.L."

Poet Lore: "Laundry Night, 1983"

The Southern Review: "Streetfighting"

Sport Literate: "My Father Shot Free Throws"

Texas Review: "The Power of the Keys"

Two Rivers Review: "Ann's Corner Store," "Phillies Fans,"
        "Soon summer will be over and the bugs will be gone,"
        "What Could Be Saved"

West Branch: "Anchor"

Yarrow: "Clever," "Handy Men," "My Father's Tomatoes"

Yellow Silk: "The Girl Who Taught Me Spanish"

I would also like to thank:

Harry Humes, terrific poet and teacher, for years of advice and
friendship. He saw various drafts of these poems and offered valu-
able suggestions.

The Constance Saltonstall Foundation for the Arts for a writing
grant which helped me to complete this book.

Also, thanks to Tony Aiello, James Longenbach, Steve Myers, Len Rob-
erts, Sean Teuton, and Jake Adam York for their help and support.

Special thanks to Karen Donaghy.

CONTENTS

Baby this town rips the bones from your back....
We gotta get out while we're young.

—Bruce Springsteen, "Born to Run"

...to arrive where we started
And know the place for the first time.

—T.S. Eliot, "Little Gidding"

THE ONE TIME I PAID ATTENTION
AT FRIDAY MORNING MASS

I dared Buddy Fisher to push
the new kid down the stairs,
bribed One-Eyed Timmy for a pair
of his sister's underwear, unaware,
until Father Flatley's homily,
I was guilty of the sin of scandal,
that it's a sin to make others sin.
In that instant, I saw the scandalous
past double my purgatory time,
movies we snuck into,
sodas we stole, the night I charmed
Karen behind the chicken coop
coming back until it was Jesus Christ
and not her father waiting
by the icy curb at midnight,
slapping the strap on His thigh,
until it was God Himself hurling me
by my neck to the back of that purgatory line,
where Brian Edwards smoked pot
with sixth graders, where Brenda Murphy
wore too much rouge and lipstick
and a low-cut, V-neck blouse,
where our mothers spread rumors
and heard every word we said.
During the Prayer for the Dead,
I renounced Satan in all his forms—
no more sneaking sips of my father's whiskey,
no more thoughts of all the girls in class
suddenly naked, lusting for me.
But then the good Father threw down
a second chalice of wine with a burp,
then Linda Dolan mouthed my name
when she leaned her head back at Communion,
eyes closed, pink tongue out,

and I lost the thought I'd never have again
as I slipped into the aisle
and marched forward to accept my host.

GEORGE

We saw him every day, shooting foul shots,
layups, jumpers from the key, his tattooed
arms a blur when he dribbled behind his back
or between his thick legs, his headband soaked,
T-shirt yellow with sweat by eight A.M.,
when we passed him on our way to school,
fixing our clip-on ties so we could look
good for Angel, Annie, and Diane.
He mumbled to himself, shouted sometimes,
all of us stopping to hear him call
the last seconds of a game, the set-up
always the same—three seconds left,
his team down one, the right side cleared out
so he could take his guy to the hole,
his thin lips a line of concentration,
head up, shoulders faking one way,
then another, his eyes always clear
so early in the morning, before he loaded trucks
at Strathmann's Lumber, before he smoked pot
at lunch and came home to two kids who weren't his,
before she slapped bills onto the kitchen table,
his rough hands steady, his spin quick
into the lane for a backdoor pass on a pick-and-roll,
his man blocked off, whole world blocked off
while he went strong to the hoop,
unstoppable, rising up to seal another win,
his sweet finger roll one perfect thing he could do.

PHILLIES FANS

Sunday mornings after church
I hustled the six blocks to Martin's,
dress shoes clacking, tie undone,
out of breath as I slid through
the doorway rich with pastry smells
and neighbors buying papers,
pickle barrel in sight, my mouth
tasting each crunch
before I'd picked up the tongs,
casting aside dark ones
too much like cucumbers,
plunging for light green
my father would slice
onto our turkey sandwiches,
saving us each an end to eat
at the start of the game,
his breathing easy then,
no wheeze or cough,
his tall glass of iced tea
even with mine those hours
we sat on the couch,
rarely talking, his thick hands
folded as if in prayer,
his mind, I see now, somewhere
he didn't like to talk about—
Korea, his cheating first wife—
our extra pickle chilled
for the seventh-inning stretch,
when we each got a half,
juices overloading our mouths,
my father showing me
how to manage all that sourness,
how to swallow it down.

JIMMY

Once a month in summer he'd cloak us
in that white sheet and shave
our heads, taper the back and sides,
check our burnt scalps for lice.
Later he'd give us cantaloupe and juice,
tell long stories of other kids
whose heads he used to shave,
how some had gone to college,
others to jail or their graves,
remind us those sweaty afternoons
that we could have it either way,
his brown eyes bloodshot, serious,
staring through us even before
we realized how wrong we could go,
or before we learned his past:
three years away for stabbing a guy,
two more for running hot cars before he
woke the hell up and learned a trade,
started cutting hair door-to-door,
then at Old Al's, finally at his own
place on Jasper. Our father told us
Listen to Jimmy, he's been there,
and he was always there those nights
we came home late, sipping black tea
on the porch he'd shared with his wife
for thirty years, calling us back with
Keep straight. Screw up and I'll know it,
shaking his crooked finger toward our house.

THE GIRL WHO TAUGHT
ME SPANISH

I stopped at the light where Pine
meets Fifth and thought of the time
I crashed my brother's car there,
the loud crack of his bumper

against that screaming priest's fender
ruining a night that was to climax
in Cookie Zuniga's swimming pool,
her parents in Ocean City with no idea

the dirty Irish boy was coming over,
who'd planned all week to make love
to their daughter. My mind drifted
from the boards in Wood Shop

to her chestnut eyes, to the long mane
of hair she twisted into a braid
the way she knew I liked it,
the glazed bench I built resembling

her parent's water-sealed dock so much
that I lay down on it and looked ahead
to Saturday—our suits heaped by the gate,
the moonlight gleaming on her

as she looked toward Heaven.
Amante! Amante! she'd moan,
calling me her lover in Spanish,
and I thought how great I'd be,

lasting until Sunday afternoon,
her parents halfway home
on the Garden State Parkway,
but then I saw her convulsing,

slapping her hands on my shoulders
like Shoemaker urging Swaps
that last quarter-mile, my words,
Hey, slow down, inaudible as she cried

Take me, take me Quixote!
the spastic moment I'd been hoping for
since I first saw her in the lunch room
approaching all too quickly,

until a horn blared from behind
and jolted me back to Philadelphia July,
children by an open hydrant,
an old man tapping the windshield

with soft pretzels, into my brother's car,
headed for an interview with Tastycake
on the Main Line. I thought hard
for a second, tried to recall the left,

then the right that would take me
to Cookie's house, wondered if she still
lived there—pink curtains in her window,
pink suit tucked into the first drawer,

if she were sunbathing on such
a lovely afternoon, shades over her eyes,
top off, her oil-slicked breasts
glistening in the sharp sun.

Shrapnel

I'm driving to work with Bruce Springsteen
screaming and my hands become smaller,
ten years old, knuckles swollen from cracking,
and I hear again my mother in the kitchen
calling my father a drunk, a sick bastard
and a drunk. I open my door enough to see
her shoulders pinned to the linoleum,
but when I shout his name he returns
to the table, to his half-eaten sandwich
and beer, and calls me to sit with him
in the sink light's fluorescent glow.
He tells me his first wife got pregnant
by a skinny Italian, and that his eyes
are bloodshot from tears, not beer,
then makes my right hand almost
invisible within his as he presses
my fingers into the shrapnel wounds
on his neck to show me just how close
I'd come to never being born.

ANT TOWN

I built them houses out of stones so they
could move from the ground, crumbed
their rooms so they'd never go hungry.
I bent blades of grass into ant-sized beds,
used twigs for a schoolhouse on the hill.
I opened the Colony Bar so they could dance,
a library, a diner, a coffee shop with really tiny espressos.
Next, a church, a town hall, a Little League field,
then ant cars and gas stations that stayed open all night.
I heard them singing at ant weddings and proms,
crying at ant funerals, moaning at the drive-in
I had to close due to neighbors' complaints.
I saw the young pitch quarters to the prison's side wall
when they should have been sleeping for school.
I saw police patrol with ant guns and clubs
chasing hookers from under the El.
I heard families in backyards, barbecuing,
toasting, together each night after work,
grandfathers holding court, cursing and laughing,
telling marvelous tales about dirt.

ONE THING THAT DIDN'T
MAKE THE PAPERS

Found on the Silver Bridge,
hung, belt around his neck:

Ready Eddie Dillaplane
from Oakdale Street;

old Jameson drinker
who never lost a fight

or a pool game at Felix's;
who coughed railroad dust

and Chesterfield phlegm.
Who shoveled walks

for nothing after storms,
whom neighbors called

when roofs leaked;
who had a '66 Barracuda

he called his only child,
and a wife who didn't drink;

who had a horseshoe scar
on his back from a fight

they had one Christmas.
And who, having outlived her,

settled his tab with Felix,
checked himself in the mirror,

said good-bye to no one,
just walked out.

THE NATURE OF MEMORY
AND FIREFLIES

In that hour between dusk and bed,
when sound was first cicadas
and neighbors on back porches,
my mother and I crept out
to chase fireflies, jar lid stabbed,
jar bottom lined with grass.
In June there were hundreds.
Oblivious as stars, they blinked
past yarrow and evening primrose
and the dead Oldsmobile
my father left us up on blocks.
She pointed when she spotted one
and I ran with splayed hands.
Her favorite moments were
watching me run back to her,
mine in the difficult passes
when our shoulders touched
and our hands cupped each other's.
I could smell the Jean Naté,
hear the starched waitress blouse
shift against her neck.

Often we cannot read the gesture
until the figure becomes background.

Once at bedtime she took a firefly
and crushed it in her palm,
smeared her finger with luciferin
to trace the lines of my cheekbones.
She held up a hand mirror
and spread the glowing lines into pools.
I cried and told her I didn't catch it for that.
I said I wished she were dead,
told her to get out, listened to her shuffle
back through the dark to her room.

Soon summer will be over and the bugs will be gone,

Marguerite says, skipping into the overgrown
field of goldenrod and yarrow,
so far from the Y's other counselors
and kids that when I look back
I can't see the building or the playground,
and I can't help thinking
it must have been a scene like this
from which a man abducted her last year,
dyed her hair red and called her
by his dead daughter's name,
and about all that might one day flood
into her consciousness, how
even though doctors told her mother
it might take years, might never come back,
I hold her hand knowing if it does
there will be nothing anyone
can do to end her grief,
and that if it all came back now,
there would be nothing more
I could do than what I'm doing.
As we head down a trail, I ask
if she's having fun, and she says *yes*
and snatches a few more ladybugs,
making over twenty for the hour,
some big with spots on each wing,
others tiny with no spots at all,
their shells flawless as her face,
her cupped hands scooping them
one by one into our bowl before
she opens the lid and sets them free.

THE YEARS WITHOUT
UNDERSTANDING

Philly July meant open hydrants,
kids in cutoffs and flip-flops,
girls in Madonna sunglasses.

It meant running from cops
who screeched around Kensington
with vise grips and angry words,

one of the boys from our ruined
neighborhood ready to soak them
with the flow they'd stop,

to shout *hosing down the pigs*
when they rushed at him,
hose 'em down

when he darted away, too quick,
diving under a fence
into the alley that would get him

halfway to Richie's Bike Shop,
where we'd laugh and smoke
and slap his back all night

on beer and crank, blazing
down roads we knew could—
but wouldn't—kill us,

breakfast at the Aramingo Diner,
more smokes, crude stories,
heavy metal on the juke box.

It meant swimming in our poverty.
Blowing off work.
Not knowing what can't last.

THE SILENT STRUMMER

From eight to eight each New Year's Day
my parents dissected the Mummers,
debating best Fancy Band, best Comic,
calling me in when the String Bands began
to watch cousin Joe lead South Philly
through "When the Saints Go Marchin' In,"
his costume alive with sequins,
his feathered boots high-stepping
past the judges and on down Market Street
while his name, our name, flashed on the screen,
enough fame to hold my father for another year,
my mother and I ready to hear again about
the day he marched: banjo player with the flu
and he the only one who fit the costume,
only one who couldn't dance or play an instrument,
the silent strummer who kept perfect time,
bad leg dipping and spinning, no sign
on his happy face of the man who'd spent
ten years of nights in the dark kitchen
cursing his boss, the stack of bills, whoever
turned on the light, his unfisted hands sparkling
while mother and I watched from the curb,
shouting to him, waving, his gleaming suit
so brilliant I had to raise my hand,
the shield I'd used for her so many nights,
pushing his bloated gut, or else hugging it,
begging him to calm down,
tightening my hold on his waist as if
I could wring the meanness out of him,
knowing I couldn't let go until I did.

ANCHOR

A grapnel, my father says before
I can ask what he's drawing,
his thick hands lifting a sketch-
book anchor into the light to show
the care he's taken—brown flakes
of rust along four hooked flukes,
a frayed rope tied to its eyehole
which looks so real I envision it
knotted to my father's waist,
retracting him when he tries to stand,
see the anchor fall through the floor
as the specked linoleum opens
to swallow him up, pulls him toward
the dimly lit bottom of his world,
where his first wife and kids, the six-
teen Koreans he killed, lurk like hungry
fish who've waited thirty years to eat,
his cries rising as silent bubbles
to the surface, where my mother and sister
have come from the parlor to watch
my father's sins devour him bit by bit,
his heart ripped out for adultery,
his legs snapped for walking out
on two young boys, each of his ribs broken
off by gaunt men with yellow faces,
yellow hands, with yellow blood pumping
through their dead yellow veins,
my father unable to look as each takes
his piece into the void, while others
claim those hazel eyes, his long
fingers, his balls, until only the rope
and the heavy iron anchor remain.

THE SOMEONE
EVERYONE KNOWS

Rainy nights in summer he'd sit
on my front stoop and play cards,
drink beer, tell lies to our fathers,
who knew as we did that
by the time he finished his fourth
he'd say again he was psychic,
able to read weather
in the black blood of crows,
see fortunes in jaw lines
and eyes, hanging his bald head
when they laughed because
his sight couldn't be denied.
It was why he anchored
Felix's bowling team,
why he was the best dart player
in the city, why everyone
was wrong when they said
what his daughter did
in the back of his work van,
stepping into the downpour,
threatening to *knock into tomorrow*
anyone who didn't take it back,
getting madder still
when our fathers laughed
and cursed and dealt him out,
knowing if they waited
long enough he'd stomp
home to look for the truth,
but find instead beer
and smokes he'd return with
and go on as before,
stripping off his wet shirt,
relaying dirty jokes
from the storm clouds,
pulling aces out of the rain.

CINDERELLA AT MIDDLE AGE

bought the feminine mystique
that a happy life lay in diaper changes,
spotless windows in a dustless home.
She traded the teenager who necked
in her father's backseat for a wife
who sleeps turned from her man,
but some nights she remembers
the promises, the sweat, the music,
his faultless blue eyes,
how he held her afterward,
windows fogged enough for her
to draw a heart for their initials,
then an arrow through the center
which pointed down like a warden
at the city they'd never leave,
even after the rug mills did,
the rendering plant, their friends,
the pleasures of motherhood great
but short-lived as money ran out
and her prince ran around with his friends,
swearing on their tiny stoop
how great he'd be someday,
when his number came in,
when he got his reward
for giving all he's got and never taking,
leaving her inside with the dinner
she'll wrap in foil and save for him,
along with the years she's lost
and how she no longer fits into things,
out of business, out of luck,
waking each morning to another midnight
with no way home from the ball.

ANN'S CORNER STORE

Ann Russell worked the night shift,
listened to Phils' games with the sound low
so her husband wouldn't hear it upstairs,
so her son wouldn't wake into the pain
he'd become from cancer, skin sliding from bone,
teeth gone, gauze hiding the scalp
once crusty from a slicked-back wave.
The boy's mitt waited by the register
while Ann bagged my candy and gum,
her chapped lips a line of worry
while Kalas called the play-by-play,
whispering into the radio
for a sign that the Phils would pull it out,
get by the Dodgers into the Series,
that the store wouldn't get robbed again
or her daughter pregnant by a corner boy,
that her son would get better
and back onto Lighthouse Field,
owning short and third, hitting clean-up,
or else die soon and get it over with,
Ann gone those tight minutes
before she came back with my change,
flipping coins into the air,
pulling one from behind her ear
before she slid them into my cupped hands.

Timmy's Eye

With its folds and fissures,
the socket looked like a cave.
It stank of antiseptic.
It couldn't stay closed.

It kept him out of school for months,
caused migraines and nausea,
nightmares of the other eye gone
and him being locked in the dark,

Timmy rarely speaking of a world
he could no longer see the edges of,
cursing the infection that strained
his half-sight until even with glasses

he needed help to dial a phone,
write his name, or turn a corner,
loud Timmy with his girlfriends
and staccato raps becoming

sad Timmy across a table,
knocking his knuckles together
when I stopped by with his work,
cursing the eye he could pop out

with a thumb and give me,
his mother for bringing in a priest
who said we were all half-seers,
who dabbed a Holy-watered finger

on Timmy's socket the way Timmy
dabbed the eye on his tongue, kissing it up
to the God he no longer thought existed
before he stuffed the buffed glass back in.

MY FATHER'S TOMATOES

My mother spent the first day
of each spring in her garden,
turning the hard dirt,
filling the burlap sack with weeds
and stones before pouring topsoil
and planting the vegetables—
carrots, beets, red peppers,
my father's Big Boy tomatoes
in their cardboard cartons.

Each night after work he'd ask
if they were ready, look out
at their beginning hefts,
until one July day my mother
handed him one and he rocked
all night on the dark porch,
eating it like an apple, now
and then adding a dash of salt.
That night there was no fighting.
No one locked herself in the bathroom,
afraid to come out.
That night, there was whistling.

He had been gone for years,
with his hard stares and pockets
full of change, but each spring
she planted them, sat them
firm and green on the sill
where they ripened and spoiled.
All summer she peeked
through the blinds, chilled a case
of Schaefer's in the refrigerator,
and listened for his truck
to settle on the stone drive.

FELIX AND THE SCHOOL DESK

He found it in his dumpster,
drawers gone, paint chipped,
curses carved into the desktop.
A little project, he said,
winking at my brother and me
on our way to shoot hoops,
sandpaper and plywood
tucked under his good arm.
Evenings he'd put George
behind the bar and get back
to the storage room,
whistling Frank Sinatra
while he rebuilt the drawers
then sanded every inch,
"Angel Eyes," "What's New?"
"It's a Lonesome Old Town,"
my brother and I watching
through the basement window
while he thumbed the inkwell
smooth, the pencil gutter,
and beneath the handles,
gliding up and down each leg,
his wife dead ten years,
his daughter trying to find
herself dancing topless in Jersey,
his hands turning raw,
dust everywhere, hacking cough,
realizing too late
he should have worn a mask,
still hawking phlegm into a napkin
when he kicked our fathers out,
still whistling Sinatra after last call,
the wee small hours of the morning
he'd tell us later, when all
good kids should be in bed,

calling us in that same afternoon
to give us the school desk,
three coats of chestnut varnish,
a matching chair.
We'd have *the world on a string,*
he said, if we studied hard,
asking again if we liked it,
if we were sure we could carry it home,
telling us to make him proud.

VISITATION B.V.M. HOLIDAY DANCE, 1982

In a low-cut dress and high heels
Linda Dolan slinked in from the snow,
eyes scanning the line of us,
thirteen and hard-up in clip-on ties
beneath the Bingo Board,
until she found her boyfriend Paul,
Dumb Paul who'd failed sixth grade,
Gross Paul who ate snot
becoming Dancing Machine Paul
under those dim basement lights,
twisting and swinging his way
into Linda's arms before Sister Joan
threw them both out. He peeked
back, smiling, as they traipsed
away toward the bullet-gray El,
sparks overloading the air
until they looked up to watch
while cars honked on both sides.
One guy flipped a finger,
another flashed his lights,
but still they held each other,
Paul pulling Linda snug to his hip
while she waved madly at the train,
both of them yelling, neither
in a hurry to look back down
and face what was coming head on.

THE POWER OF THE KEYS

When Sister told our class
how Jesus, by dying, gave us
the Kingdom of heaven's keys,
I saw again the keys we stole
from Father Flatley to guzzle
church wine, I looked over
to see Buddy Fisher steal
his brother's car keys,
his father's liquor cabinet keys,
I heard the key to the math test
crinkling up Tommy Ryan's sleeve,
going on like that until
Sister wrote the power of the keys
on the cracked blackboard,
told us there was no offense
Christ would not pardon,
no man for whom He wouldn't
open *the gates of forgiveness,*
staring at Billy McCook
who spray painted on walls,
at Benny Shaw who broke windows,
working her way to Annie Palazzo
with her lipstick and gum,
Joan Keegan with her perfume,
finally to me because she knew
my father once chased my mother
with a knife, she could sense
his hard heart spreading to me
even though I sat eight hours a day
under the heavy cross,
recited the Our Father and Hail Mary
at Friday morning Mass,
even though I knelt and rose on cue
and marched to the altar
for my communion host,
she knew it was her job

to fight wickedness and call us back
to faith, to remind us
this was no set of house keys
she was talking about,
this was *eternal liberation,*
longer than any R-rated movie,
better than any kiss,
spreading her arms to emphasize
the vastness of Christ's mercy,
making us look to the nails
driven forever into His wrists
and feet, see the blood
dripping from the Crown of Thorns,
making us close our eyes
to imagine that pain,
the lance ripping our sides,
muscle tearing from bone
under the dense weight of sin,
telling us to stretch out our arms,
to taste that holy blood,
to open our still-living souls
so that we could reside with Christ,
whose grace has saved us.

Elegy for T.L.

The El's catwalk called to us
while we passed quarts

of Schaefer's someone stole.
Fifty feet up, it stretched

beyond our broken places
in both directions.

I was second to make it to the top.
I stared at your dark form

and streetlights even with our heads,
saw you tightroping the catwalk

straight out of your life
toward the houses of the rich.

You didn't once look down.
You didn't hold the rail.

The only sounds our feet
shuffling the metal walk.

You fell so quietly
no one else knew you were gone.

NOCKAMIXON LAKE

Far from the city that closed on us
like a fist all June and July,
away for a few minutes
from the family party
and its cooler of iced Millers,
I pencil dove into the lake,
my body stiff as a nail
as it cut through water
that darkened as I sank,
bubbles rushing up like smoke
as I sliced down and down,
pushing up with my palms,
driving deeper into what
we never felt in those rowhomes
set along greasy avenues—
not freedom exactly, but something
like it—a boundlessness
my lungs ached against past
mud-silted sunnies and bass,
beneath the staccato of outboards
and screaming children,
my father's black lungs drifting away
with my mother's black eyes
and her cries in the hallway at night,
the Sisters of Saint Joseph
vanishing when I closed my eyes
to their Bible passages
and the prayers we said by rote,
sinking past drowned logs
until my foot wedged between rocks.

On the bottom of the lake
I hung like a balloon fighting
to free itself from a greedy boy's hand,
flailing my arms in the cloud I made,
squinting against the vise closing

in on my temples, looking up
to the sky's white rim along the surface
where like a bird a beer can fell,
the twig of a cigarette, and then my father,
who couldn't swim, fell face first
toward the last bubbles I could push
from my nose and mouth.
He held his arms straight out
as if across a canyon, roaring to me,
touching first my hair, then my face,
my eyes leading him to the foot he freed
from the leather basketball sneaker
he'd worked overtime to pay for.
When he patted the back of my leg,
I pushed off and burst toward
the exhausted air above the lake,
my arms churning like oars,
thinking even then only of myself,
not knowing until later how
he'd known where to look for me,
how he'd calmed everyone
before he dove by swearing
that he would not come up alone.

THREE HOUSES,
THREE DOGS

My father came each night
to tuck me in, creaking down
our hall in work boots
he always wore, laces undone,
the stale mix of Schaefer's
and Pall Malls waking me
into the darkness he lived in,
my mother in bed,
my sister out, him whistling
for hours to Jim Reeves
or listening to news radio.
Years passed like that,
grammar and middle school,
three houses, three dogs,
him rising each five A.M.
to wire boats at the Navy Yard,
never telling me what
he thought about those nights
before he tousled my hair
with root-thick fingers
and leaned down to kiss my cheek.

HE SOLD ME MY FIRST CAR
FOR TWO HUNDRED BUCKS

Even on summer's hottest days
we knew we'd pass Blind Ed
on our way to shoot hoops
at The Lot, that by noon he'd
be deep into one of his junkers,
checking plugs and points,
hoses and valves, leaning close
to the blurred flywheel
to set the idle speed, reaching
surely for each part even though
cataracts took most of his sight,
left him with shadows for a family,
no money in the bank, dead
cars scattered on his lawn.
We knew to say his name softly,
to approach only after he extended
his greasy hand, which we shook
in spite of the awkwardness we felt
when he talked about nothing,
about school and our parents,
the loud jeeps that raced our street
at night, no one able to look too long
at his roaming pupils and blue irises
gone white, or at the hands shaking deep
in his pockets, as though he might
pull out something other than smokes
or a buck for one of us to rake his leaves,
something he just had to show us—
a watch or ring, a vanishing coin—
some small thing to take with us
and pass back and forth like a ball.

SNOW HITCHERS

Beneath the El that cast blackness
over everything, before babies
and jail terms and jobs we hate,
we huddled at Jasper and Lehigh
until a car slid past, then ran
to grab its bumper and tuck our legs
underneath, ease ourselves
onto the snow-covered street
to get dragged the hundred feet
to Emerald, bouncing over
potholes, ice chunks, and salt,
scraping over clear patches of road.
Two at a time we'd go, our bodies
soaked with oil and black slush
by the time we pushed off
at Griffin's Deli, then raced back
to the corner, checking each other
for cuts because we were too numb
to feel anything, too dumb
to go home when we were hurt
because we couldn't miss swishing
through our neighborhood,
below our mothers staring out windows,
past our fathers in Tinney's Bar,
below brake lights and turn signals
we prayed the driver would never use
while we skidded behind,
taking it all in, hoping more
snow would fall so we could hitch
rides for weeks, up and down
each street, past everyone we knew,
our bodies smashed together
at the shoulders, chained
tires inches from our feet.

DIGGING FOR SUMMER: 1986

First Griffin's Deli, then Panno's Pizza,
then all the houses on Jasper Street,
each sidewalk getting us five bucks
closer to what we were saving for,
our shovels scraping pitted concrete,
dreams of Jersey shore summers
thawing us in blue-black December,
tree limbs like wires, snow clumped
on our boots, hats, and gloves
while in our heads
danced girls around a campfire,
loving Billy's bleeding sax,
gushing for my Gibson guitar,
our hair slicked back,
both smoking after months
of freezing our asses off,
suddenly musical, stealing grace
from the surface of the waves,
pulling lyrics from smoke and wind,
rising into our groove
like when we straighten
our backs to let the ache out,
dipping left and right,
Billy singing Springsteen
while I jammed on shovel-guitar,
blood warming our faces,
cars rattling by on chains
as if to remind us why
we were out there,
as if we could forget,
both sixteen and ready,
our futures calling,
two blocks left before dark.

WILDWOOD

You're under your car all night,
fightin' with the tranny,
tightenin' the brake band,

adjuster   servo diaphragm,
so she'll stop slippin',
shift slick and smooth,

get you outta Philly
to where you need to go,
which is Wildwood

wild waves   wild women
walkin' the boardwalk
in next-to-no clothes.

Anything goes in Wildwood,
where you stay with friends
get stupid   dance wild

sing the same three records:
Bruce Springsteen,
Don McLean, Billy Joel

when he was good,
and you're real good,
always good in Wildwood,

where you make a new start—
part your hair on the side,
flip it back   say you got style—

pile up your clothes
and burn 'em in the sand,
hand out beers and toast

New start, new start—
that no-style guy was the old you—
and you gotta do somethin' crazy

pretty quick
cause you only got three days,
and it pays to move fast

in Wildwood   wild nights
wild days call for plays
that ain't in the book,

and you look so cool
you get a chill
when you pass a mirror—

Gap shorts and shirt,
two hundred dollar shoes,
and the hat you've wanted

for years. You're fearless
reckless   makin' a pass
at every girl on the boardwalk

'cause you want to be
under it   gettin' it,
gettin' what you don't know,

but you know you gotta go
to the end of the pier,
get a new beer, and hear

the band in the grandstand
playin' reggae then—heyhey—
you spot your kinda girl

on the Tilt-a-Whirl—
wild girl   crazy girl
hands-above-her-head girl,

even through the sharpest turns—
and it burns you up
to see her lean into the guy

she's with—all biceps
triceps   his whole body
one big cep—'cept

he ain't got no neck,
and you can't respect
no man with no neck

sure as you can't beat him
in a fight   and you might
be in the middle of one

if you keep starin' at his girl,
so you stop starin'
and they're still twirlin',

and every girl in Wildwood
looks good to you now,
except they're all holdin' hands

with someone else.
Your friends are holdin'
more than hands   holdin' bodies

holdin' breath   holdin' breasts
they'll tell you about all week
at work, and you gotta work

so you gotta hear their stories,
and they're gonna ask for yours
and you don't want to talk

about no seashells, cause
you're in Wildwood   wild fun
wild sun burnin' your back,

when what you really want
are rope burns   rug burns
somethin' to show off at work,

but nothin' you try works
so you duck into Madam Marie's
for five bucks of advice—

her crystal ball never lies—
and your eyes are like baseballs
when you look around the place:

fake bats   stuffed rats
black cats sleepin' on shelves
next to autographs she's gotten

from dead guys—Bogie, The Duke,
Elvis when he was young—
you're young   got all your teeth,

don't go heavy on booze, but
you couldn't get lucky in Las Vegas.
Marie calls for silence   patience

looks intense   all that incense
is makin' you dizzy, and Marie's
in a tizzy, up against that ball

like she sees years of bad news,
and you get the blues just thinkin'
'bout it. When the smoke clears,

Marie peers into that thing,
jingles her rings and tells you
to *look, look for yourself,*

but all you see is smoke
like you saw the whole
ride down in your rearview,

and when it starts to clear
you think you see yourself
on a boat   in a house

in a Japanese car, and you know
it's you cause of your hat—
there's only one hat like that—

but there's nobody else in the picture,
and now there's nobody else
in the room, 'cause Marie's

gone with your five bucks
and your luck's the same
as it was, rotten, and it's gotten

no better in Wildwood
wild screams wild dreams
in every head, in every bed

and yours are gonna stay
in your car, 'cause it's too far
to walk back to your friend's

and you're too drunk
to drive, plus you can't even
remember the address.

You and Irene

It's Saturday night, senior year.
Everyone off someplace warm:
basement parties, barrel fires.

Kensington Avenue is all
piss and beer, empty stores,
stale air trapped beneath the El

you'll take tonight to meet Irene
at the Devon movie theater,
the El you used to climb with friends

to beat the fare, shimmying
a beam ten feet until you reached
a service ladder, then climbing

the last forty toward South Street
or the Spectrum, rising into
the station's fluorescent glow,

never looking below until
Wild C fell into a broken back,
you watching from the catwalk

as he flipped once and landed
on his head, doctors sure
he wouldn't make the week

but he lasted three months,
head twice its normal size
and purple, never coming out

of the dark, the way light never
cuts through the El tracks
on Kensington, where it's always night,

rusted steel sky hovering,
shadows falling from everywhere,
slashing the wet crosses

above old Frankie and his wine,
and Richie from the bike shop,
guarding hookers asleep

in doorways until horns honk,
pulling at Ann Russell
as she dies of a heart attack,

and Joel Frazier as he chops
crank on a hand mirror,
and it sweeps up you too

as you shuffle toward the steps
to Irene and the movies,
Wild C still falling, your arm

still flailing the air because
the past is never past,
it's always present,

and you hope something
funny is playing tonight,
something you and Irene

can laugh about at the Melrose
over coffee and smokes,
little jukebox crooning,

neon lights lining the ceiling,
casting out shadows,
streaming down onto your booth.

CLEVER

When a man came to my door asking
about the Chevette by the curb,
I told the truth: cracked cylinder head,
bad brakes, a timing belt that could

snap any day, and I expected him
to be like the rest, to say thank you
and leave, but instead he asked
to take a look, said he had a friend

who was clever with cars, who'd fix
anything for fifty bucks and a beer.
He offered 150, twice as much
as the junk yard, so we shook on it,

then walked back to the house
for title and plates. I kept on
about extra fuses in the glove,
told him how the seats recline

all the way back, not sure
if I should mention how
Robin Richie taught me that
our senior year, or how

she kicked a dent in the dash
that night on Snake Road
when we were finally alone,
when I let her hair down

and buried my face in her breasts,
not sure he would care to know
how our flesh melted
to the seats, or how her neck smelled,

sweet strawberry scent that wafted
over the plastic Mary hung
from the mirror, over our knotted
shoes and sweaty hump of clothes,

over our stiff bodies,
out the window and down the road
that led to Visitation Church
and then to our homes,

side-by-side tenements
with yards linked by a gate
my father chained shut
when he caught me sneaking in

one four A.M., Robin's black bra
under my arm, his beer on my breath,
my shirt out, her bedroom light
snapping off just as our door clicked shut.

CONVERSION

When Sister told us the human heart
grows heavy and hard from sin,
each curse adding another ounce,
each lie another squeeze
inside the sinner's black chest
until he repents or drops dead
from the weight, I looked out
the barred window wondering
how long my father had left,
knowing it was only a matter
of time before he fell down
the one-way road to Hell,
as Sister called it, knowing
my father said more than once
that he'd never repent, that if God
had any guts He'd repent
for leaving my father an orphan
at fourteen, for the year in Korea
he keeps reliving in his dreams,
for the shakes he steadies with booze,
arthritic knee he quiets with pills,
reminding me once that God
didn't put food on our table,
didn't pay our bills, rising
into the smoky cave of that kitchen
to say that God's never helped him at all,
chalking up his few breaks to luck,
pointing to the Coral Street woman with twins—
one deaf, the other half-blind—
asking *Where was God for her?*
me unable to answer before he said,
See what I mean, boy? Do you see?
spreading his arms until he filled
that cold room with his emptiness,
looking up past the stained ceiling,
past the attic and cracked roof,

past the few stars of that smog-dim city,
looking all the way to God to tell Him
He could save His sacred breath
because there was nothing He could do
to change his mind, he was a lost soul,
a heathen, a Cardiac Christian
who'd shout *Sweet Jesus, I'm sorry*
just before he died and not one second before.

MY FATHER SHOT
FREE THROWS

From the window I watched
him go through his routine:
deep knee bends, two dribbles,
a long drag from his Pall Mall,
a few backspins of the ball
before he was gone into the void
of that rim, the blank space
he lived in for an hour each night,
free of us nagging him
to quit the smokes and heavy drink,
free of my mother over his shoulder
when he spat blood,
rubbing his back, crying
when he refused to go for X rays,
free of all but the constant
wheeze in his lungs that kept
him nearly always out of breath,
that kept him awake,
sent him downstairs for water
then out to the drive,
my father easing into it,
a few lay-ups, some jumpers,
always a neighbor's light on,
always the hacking cough,
the soft hiss off the boards,
always the underhanded shot.

SNAPSHOT

Rita Lehman's chasing a bouquet
of wildflowers in the background,
some blues and yellows settling
at the base of St. Michael's stairs,
some browns at my brother's feet
as he poses between our parents,
smiling, the black robe fluttering
behind him. His head's turned
slightly to the right, toward
the far end of the school yard,
where the rest of his life waits
with Jimmy Cook, the pool shark,
and one-eyed Timmy, with the line
of whores from Front Street,
Candy, Dolores, Rebecca-
with-the-false-teeth, all of them
waving him toward the piss-stink
of abandoned houses, holding out
paint thinner and Schaefer's,
stripped wires of stolen cars,
holding up our parents' checkbook,
bags of new clothes, beer cases,
pounds of pot, each laughing
after a long hit from a joint,
blowing smoke rings toward
face-shaped clouds, one long
and skinny with his big ears,
another darker, the silhouette
of his junkie lover, whom
he'd beat and have babies with,
three smaller ones floating by
for each kid they'd lose to the courts,
an oblong eight for his time in prison,
a Roman ten for his stab wounds, thin
one for the years he'd live past thirty,

a half-oval floating by like the stone
over his Forest Hills grave,
row twenty-seven, plot twelve,
where my parents insisted
on staying after the funeral,
until the flowers were stripped away
and the workers cranked him down.

STREETFIGHTING

When my sister fell into the house crying,
holding her face, I knew even before
she pulled back her hands
what her boyfriend Benny had done.

I ran upstairs to get my sneakers
even though it was nine o'clock
on a school night, almost time for bed,
my mother'd told me minutes before,

my sister's boyfriend sixteen,
me twelve, wishing I'd paid more attention
to my father's boxing lessons—
left hand over right, feet shoulder-width apart,

his slippers shuffling around that closet
of a kitchen while I followed him
in slow looping circles—same moves
I made after I raced out the front door

wanting someone to stop me,
mix of who I was and thought I had to be
swirling in my head since he left us
in inner-city Philadelphia, where

any day my mother could get mugged,
my sister raped, any day I could get
my ass kicked defending them in a fight,
anger lasting me only long enough

for one good crack to the jaw
before I fell back into myself
and felt the punches rain down,
the kicks, the shots to the stomach

that knocked the wind out of me
like the sight of his truck pulling away,
not once looking into the rearview
before he hit the gas and screeched

beneath the Market-Frankford El,
pain I swallowed until I'd let nothing
hurt us, clenching and unclenching
my fists as I walked toward where

I knew Benny would be, same fists
I flung into my father's gut
those nights their voices rose,
still feeling the crown of my head

against his ribs, still seeing the glint
of florescent light off his belt buckle
while my mother locked herself
in their bedroom and called him

a crazy drunk, and with all this
I found Benny laughing with his friends,
one leg up on a car fender,
one hand wrapped around a beer can,

with all this I charged at him
and plowed my head into his chest,
swung at his jaw and neck,
seeing not Benny's but my father's face,

unmistakable—the bloodshot eyes,
the scar plowing across his forehead—
and I flailed all of my weight at him
as many times as I could, roundhouses,

jabs, hooks, hitting and getting hit,
I'm sure, but not feeling any of it,
our neighbors circled around us,
some cheering, some with crossed arms

while blood flowed from our faces
and hands, sprayed onto houses and cars,
onto our shirts and sneaks and jeans,
before it mixed with the glass-littered ground.

LAUNDRY NIGHT, 1983

Some nights she'd throw their clothes
into the car's trunk and take off,
hair rolled tight, no note, mother
of two teenagers gone for hours
down Oakdale and Albert Streets,
Frankie Avalon singing "Venus" above
the old Rambler's tapping valves
as it machine-gunned past Griffin's Deli
and Garzone's Funeral Home,
past Visitation Church and School,
her unringed fingers tapping the wheel,
her breathing easier by the time
she made the tricky right at Kip Street
and swished into her usual spot
outside Soapy Suds, almost forgetting
her husband had left, she couldn't find a job,
almost outrunning the family
she broke from when they said
he was no good, "A Perfect Love,"
"Don't Throw Away All Those Teardrops"
coming back from the kitchen
of their first apartment.
                                    And now
it turned out her family was right,
a scar on her cheek the proof,
and the stack of bills, the nightmares
of police coming to take her children,
her house, her dog, leaving her nothing—
and so the fears flowed
while she sorted the brights and darks,
knowing there was no getting clean
after months of crying herself
to sleep, no point in scrubbing
the stains ground into their lives,

grass stains, blood stains
so much a part of her they might
as well have been skin, no way
to make her children look presentable
on what he sent every other week,
her own clothes stretched like
her sagging arms and breasts,
her shoes *so holy they could be saints,*
little joke she told the washer
when she dropped in a load of whites,
"Bobby Socks to Stockings"
coming back after twenty years
when she measured the powdered soap,
the fabric softener, the bleach,
always the bleach, which still stung
her nose after the cycle was done,
when she pulled out the clothes
and held them overflowing in her arms.

HANDY MEN

Nine hours a day for two days
my father and I rebuilt the john,
ripped out cabinet and mirror,
towel bar, shower rod,
tore down drop ceiling and walls,
my father catching a smoke
and an inning of the Phils
before we cut the paneling,
another smoke before we slapped
their backs with adhesive
and pressed them to the studs,
sweat sliding from his pompadour,
arm stretched to tack in the tops
as if he were tacking planes again
to the ceiling of my boyhood room,
those Mustangs and Hellcats
hovering while I dozed
to the lull of my parents' voices.
One panel at a time, we worked
our way around the room,
negotiating heat vent and toilet tank,
light switch and sink,
my father teaching me
to align the fake tiles,
to hide mistakes behind trim,
making me repeat his lessons
later over pizza and wings,
so I'd be set for my own house,
which he'd visit and inspect,
his head nodding, bad leg
stretched over a chair,
his words becoming mine
in the room we'd take on next.

HEARTWOOD

Beneath the shagbark hickory, she removes
wet gloves, shoves them into her pockets,
blows steaming air into her hands.
She stands as her father never stood,
deep in woods, swinging an ax to break
what will heat her house all winter.

She sees her father back home, reading
in his window chair, in the neighborhood
he swore his children would never see,
the one he'd grown up in, hookers and bars,
no trees, abandoned houses and stores.
She sees snow piling up there as it does here,

thick wet flakes he'll send her out to shovel
from front sidewalk and back, then make cocoa
for when she came in, his steam-fogged glasses
making them both laugh. She hears the cough,
smells the Pall Malls, feels what comes next
rise up in her like the ax she lifts above her head

and drives down through the heartwood
it takes two or three heaves to crack open,
stubborn, dead wood she curses until her hands
become raw, and her neck and face and feet,
until all of the wood is split and stacked
and the first armful is hissing in the stove.

THE MAN WHOSE WIFE HAD DIED

Felix wanted to keep it perfect,
so twice a week that summer
he pushed his mower with its rattle
and blue smoke around the lawn,
short white sleeves, dress shoes,
pants creased as if for church.
His belly rolled over his belt
as he rolled around the yard,
all the steps planned—
slow dip beneath clothesline,
figure-eight around pines—
each stride smooth enough
not to startle finches at their feeders
or crook the Irish eight-piece cap,
his back-steps past lawn chairs
easy all the way to the garden,
where he cut the engine
and picked crabgrass by hand,
then sat by the fence. How long
he stayed there each morning,
still as her empty chair, staring
beyond lettuce and rhubarb,
the grass relentlessly green.

Things Like This Happen
All The Time

Meet the woman who collected cans
in a thumping metal shopping cart.
Notice her stray dog, her radio.

Meet the boys who wanted to rob her.
See their school, St. Michael's,
all steeple and stained glass, bells.

Late spring: more light each day.
Friday: people leaving early
for Sea Bright or Avalon or Ocean City.

Feel the oak pews the boys sat in.
Smell the rear corner where she stood
through homily and communion.

This is what she smelled like:
the bar dumpster whose scraps
and empties she lived on.

And note where the boys hid:
between delivery trucks while
cars raced Kensington Avenue.

She did not hear them approach
over gravel and broken glass.
She threw cans over her shoulder.

Remember that they were not
content to take the cart. They
pulled her from the dumpster.

They smacked her around,
dared her to fight back,
kicked her legs and her dog.

Taste her blood on your tongue.
Think of what you would do.
Remember: There were four of them.

Here is where she picked up her dog
and ran into the street at a busy time.
There is the boy who stood stone-like.

The direction the others ran.
It was an old man who took the radio.
There were many who fought for the cans.

CHRISTMAS

Two years after his death my father
still comes to snap me awake,
bringing back his burning hours,
high fever, delusions, and then release,
when we stood in the wake of what
we'd prayed for saying good-bye,
mother stroking his hair,
some small death happening in all of us,
his last words, *I love you*, the same
as our last each night before bed,
sending me ahead however
many years to when it's our turn,
you over me, or me over you,
nights like this precious,
your body firm and warm in my arms
with the window open and the scattered noises.
Some nights are easy and I sleep like this.
Some bring morphine, soiled sheets,
her whispering his name, my name,
over and over. You were there.
We need to talk about it:
how one of us will live without the other.

HALFIES IN PHILADELPHIA
AND THE RITUAL OF DESIRE

Twenty years later I find half a tennis ball
in the woods and return for a while
to that cramped geography at the other
end of my life, empty mills and El tracks
casting shadows we did not yet feel on our backs.
Our fingers curled around halfies' ruined edges,
mop handle bats twitched within the fists of friends
now gone to drugs or crime or some other darkness,
a shot to the first floor a single, to the second, a double,
the third, a triple, the roof an elusive home run,
no bases to trot around, home plate a chalked square.
Radio pounding, tire hiss, acrid smell of smoke
from coal cars clacking past our dead neighborhood
on the way to somewhere far from Perlstein Glass
and the rank, back alley of our failures. Our fathers
worked hard for nothing wages, came home to beer,
a hot shower, a hot meal. They did not talk much,
nor did we those afternoons we tested each other
with trick pitches—flying saucers, German helmets—
tapping aside what we did not like until we strode
into one with a vicious uppercut, trying
to lift it above our little lives into the air
where no birds flew, where the wind could catch it
and pull it onto the roof, evanescent and free.

Fresh Start: Staining the Pool Deck

Again I set aside half the day
to put another coat on the pool deck,
again the gloves, again the stain can
and the beer can, fingers only half
an ache because I passed the brush
between hands each twenty strokes,
one useful thing my father taught me
while I whitewashed the hall steps
in the rowhouse I left half my life ago,
house of nicotine and dog hair,
house he left us alone in
on a street of houses rotting
against each other like teeth,
house so far from this half-acre
I have to squeeze my eyes to see it—
ripped linoleum, cracked walls,
dirt cellar of rats and mold,
nights of yelling behind doors....

Half a life later I'm trying to get
to the next day, after the deck dried,
when we swam in finally blue water.
I'm trying to work the float into this,
and the inner tubes, the handstands,
the red and yellow beachball.
Enough about my long-dead father,
food stamps, government cheese.
What about my wife asleep
cross-legged in the Adirondack chair,
my daughter's brilliant pink suit,
the gray fox panting at the woods' edge?
And what about how cold the beer was,
how bright the sun over the crab apple tree
when I sank to the soundless bottom

and watched my daughter's kicking?

Lucky are those who make it through
doors just before the locks click shut,
who turn corners and lose the way back.
Lucky those who get new starts:
Richard Wright after Memphis,
Dylan at Royal Albert Hall,
Raskolnikov crying at Sonia's knees,
so ashamed he cannot look up.

Daniel Donaghy holds a B.A. from Kutztown University, an M.A. from Hollins College, and an M.F.A. in creative writing (poetry) from Cornell University. He is currently completing a Ph.D. in English at the University of Rochester. His poems have appeared in *New Letters, The Southern Review, Poet Lore, Cimarron Review, Texas Review, Commonweal, Image, West Branch,* and other journals. He has received fellowships from the National Endowment for the Humanities, the Constance Saltonstall Foundation for the Arts, and the Cornell Council for the Arts. He lives in Spencerport, New York, with his wife and daughter.